PIANO
solos

NARADA ARTISTS

Hal Leonard Publishing Corporation

7777 West Bluemound Road P.O. Box 13819 Milwaukee, WI 53213

This songbook is a companion piece to the Narada recording PIANO SOLOS.
The album contains the selections as performed by their composers. Compact discs
and cassettes are available in fine record stores worldwide or by writing:

Hal Leonard Publishing Corporation
P.O. Box 13819, Milwaukee, WI 53123 USA

Learning Through Music: A Commitment from Narada

Narada and its artists endorse the work of the
National Coalition for Music Education, which consists of:

Music Educators National Conference (MENC)
National Academy of Recording Arts and Sciences (NARAS)
and National Association of Music Merchants (NAMM)

These three non-profit groups have joined together to create awareness
and focus attention on the need of including music instruction as
an essential element of a well-rounded education.

For more information on the Coalition please write or call:

Music Educators National Conference
1902 Association Drive, Reston, VA 22091
703-860-4000

Cover photography by Mike Huibregtse
Design by Connie Gage and Eric Lindert

PIANO *solos*

CONTENTS

INTRODUCTION

By Marienne Uszler

Any musical instrument makes magic possible. The magic happens when someone plays that instrument, experiencing discovery and creation. In some sense, each instrument is a challenge. It says, "Touch me, and see what you can do." But each instrument also promises a kind of friendship, suggesting shared, very personal experiences. It says, "Only you and I will chart the paths that we will follow. Only you and I will understand why we explore in exactly the way we do." The rapport between instrument and player is unique. It is much more personal than non-players suppose.

For many people, the piano is *the* instrument. Why this is so will always be somewhat mysterious, just as every attraction is part enigma. But some of the piano's magnetism is unmistakable. It has a sweeping range; eighty-eight pitches represent a world of individual choices as well as another kaleidoscopic world of pitch combinations. The pedals enhance sounds just as much as they sustain them, effects so far-reaching that Anton Rubinstein is credited with declaring the pedals the "soul" of the piano. The piano seems easy to play; touching a key produces sound in a way that is immediately accessible to anyone — even the youngest child. The piano is responsive in a way that other keyboards are not; the greater the energy, the bigger and richer the sound. And, on the piano, the player is able to be — simultaneously — both soloist and background. While that sometimes proves challenging, meeting that challenge is richly satisfying.

When someone decides to play the piano, or to take lessons, it is always with the hope that the magic will happen for them, that the piano will become another "voice" with which to speak, if only to delight in another personal reverie and fantasy. If that person is young, the vision of what lies ahead is a combination of excitement and curiosity. If the person is older, the hope is often for something that will prove relaxing and enriching. In either case, the search is for something elusive. And it must be a search, one undertaken with effort, care, and determination. The rewards and discoveries are in proportion to the honesty and quality of the venture.

Today many adults are investing time and money in piano instruction. The reasons are as variable as the people but, ultimately, most concede that they do so "just for myself." For some that may mean a wistful return to an enterprise begun in childhood. For others, it is a way to stretch the self, to go beyond mundane tasks. For many, it also represents an entrance into the world of the performing arts, to seek there what cannot be found in ordinary recreation, sports, or reading. Making music is self-expression freed from the search for words and the weighing of specific meanings. It is exhilarating. It is fulfilling. It is deeply personal.

Playing the piano can be done alone — on quiet nights, in moments of tension, through hours of musing. Playing the piano can be friendly and useful — backing up a sing-along, leading hymns at church, or playing duets. Playing the piano may be a special sort of sharing — providing pleasure and inspiration for those who listen. Playing the piano is a way of recreating music already written — connecting with composers past and present. Playing the piano releases music that arises spontaneously from the secret self. Improvising does not have to be fancy or complicated. It requires only a readiness to try, to experiment, to step out over the edge.

Piano keys can be keys in the real sense. They can open doors that reveal surprising vistas. They can unlock reservoirs of untapped energies. Touch them. The magic can happen for you.

Pianist Marienne Uszler is a professor in the Department of Keyboard Studies at the University of Southern California. She is coauthor and editor of *The Well-Tempered Keyboard Teacher*, articles and reviews editor for *American Music Teacher* and contributing editor for *The Piano Quarterly*.

MICHAEL JONES

My fascination with the piano began when I was 2. I was captivated by the smell of the wood, the smooth, cool texture of the ivory keys, the sensation of the notes and the feeling they created as they resonated through my body. In time I learned other instruments, such as the clarinet and the saxophone, but I felt satisfied only when I played them with an orchestra or a band. The piano, on the other hand, was complete in itself. With it, I *was* the orchestra.

However, after years of classical training and quiet evenings of improvisation, I eventually set aside my piano playing and yielded to the more practical concerns of building a career as an educator and consultant. Yet my love for the instrument never waned, and often I could be found musing at the keyboard. One evening in the lobby of a restored hotel, an older gentleman found me at the piano and shared my astonishment at the sounds that flowed from it.

Later, I explained to him my role as a consultant and my reluctance to leave such an orderly and rational world for the more mysterious realms of piano playing. His eyes flashed intensely. "But who will play your music?" he asked.

I heeded his words. It was the piano that most excited me and invigorated my heart. Once again I tapped the wellspring, allowing my fingers to dance over the keys and giving myself over to an adventure that would have no beginning and no end.

An abridged version of Aspen Summer has been included in this songbook due to the length of the original recording on PIANO SOLOS by Michael Jones.

Photo by V. Tony Hauser

SPENCER BREWER

I do not remember a time in my life when I was not somehow influenced by the piano. I started playing at the age of 8, an age when many children begin playing, whether they want to or not. By 10, I was already experimenting with it as a source of creativity and an outlet for my personal expression.

More than a musical instrument, I found the piano to also be a friend and confidant which I could turn to when I needed to work through my thoughts and emotions. As the years have passed, after owning nearly 400 pianos and restoring or tuning thousands of

others, I look at the piano and appreciate it for its steadfastness and its character, for its ability to patiently absorb any feeling or idea that I bring to the bench, no matter how complex or trivial. The piano does not argue or contradict. Instead, it openly receives my feelings and emotions without passing judgment, and it responds with understanding, compassion and tenderness. I feel blessed to have had such a wonderful friend throughout my life.

Photo by Tom Liden

Michael Gettel

I was 9 when the moving truck delivered our first family piano to our home in Colorado. It was an upright, and it took up an entire wall in our living room. As my love for playing grew, a few years later my parents surprised me on my birthday with a very special gift — a new Yamaha grand.

As if this were not enough of a surprise, my parents had the new piano placed *in my room*, which is where I discovered it when I came home from school that day. This required *substantial* furniture rearranging — even the acquisition of a smaller bed. (I spent the first week, in fact, sleeping underneath my new instrument.) From that moment, I literally *lived* in my room. My parents and I shared a bedroom wall and, to their chagrin, I usually played late into the night. Even after I left for college, I always looked forward to coming home and getting reacquainted with those special keys.

That was a decade ago . . .

Last spring, a moving truck arrived at my home in Seattle. While I was away teaching at school, a well-cared-for Yamaha grand was moved into my studio.

These keys know every note I've ever played — my very heart and soul.

Welcome home . . .

Photo by M. P. Curtis

Wayne Gratz

Although there are many relationships experienced during our lifetimes, I have found only one that remains consistent — the one I share with my family. Members of my family are always nearby to share the joys and disappointments of each growing year.

The piano, I have come to realize, has also become a part of my family. I vividly remember receiving my first piano at the age of 5. It was as though my mother and father had just brought home a new brother or sister. At this time, little did I know that this instrument of creation was going to be the center of my life. Like members of my family, the piano has been a nurturing companion, a friend and an inspiration for creation. It has become a part of me — forever.

Photo by Allen-Knox

IRA STEIN

The best way for me to express or relate my emotions is through playing the piano. It is my voice, a direct extension of my heart. The whole process began when I was 10, when I would practice my Bach or Haydn instead of skateboarding with friends.

Later I began to improvise, the truest form of self-expression. At such moments, my fingers touch down on the keys and I no longer have to think. A dynamic link of the soul and hands occurs that may continue for hours. It pauses only for occasional breaks of silence, and it ends only when the feeling has been fully conveyed.

When I'm happy or peaceful, I can rejoice in the pure sensual pleasure of the sounds and melodies that I can produce. And, when I'm sad or angry, improvising on the piano can be healing by the cathartic release of my emotions, and comforting by the sound of music that I have never before imagined, which rises up to my ears. Sometimes I'll play something that pleases me so much that I'll repeat it over and over again until I can't forget it. It grows into a form, and a song is born.

Photo by Irene Young

KOSTIA

I was 4 years old when I received my first piano — a 1937 Wolkenhauer upright. My parents had sent it as a gift from East Germany, where they lived and worked. My home was in Russia, with my grandmother in a tiny apartment in St. Petersburg.

This piano was the center of life in our home. Even my pet rooster, Peter, used its lid as his favorite perch, the place where he would listen as I played.

This piano was not simply a piece of furniture. I feel it had a life of its own. To touch her ivory keys was to communicate with her. She was the source of the most profound heart-and-soul relationship I have ever had.

I am grateful to have studied under two of Russia's great master teachers, Vladimir Nielsen and Tamara Karetkina, who encouraged a sense of reverence for the relationship between pianist and piano. From them I learned that people with great technical skills may be able to play very fast or perform complex passages, but they may be only pushing keys to express their ego — not to make music.

To the musician, the piano is more than a box with keys and wires; it is a part of music itself. When I play, the piano becomes part of me, and I become more than myself. It is a bridge to the dimension where music exists, and it takes time and talent to be in tune with the piano — to be in tune with music. It is a mystery, I know, but it is a wonderful mystery, and my life as a musician is devoted to understanding it more deeply.

Photo by Dick Zimmerman Studios/Dick Zimmerman

NANCY RUMBEL

My involvement with music began with the piano. This long, horizontal, inviting mystery sat in our family's living room where my mother would teach piano lessons by day and play music to put the children to sleep at night. Finally, when I could reach it, I began exploring its phenomenal capabilities, quickly prompting my mother to direct my wild improvisations into some sort of form and structure. I played all those childhood classics, from *The Spinning Song* and *Minuet in G* to *Fur Elise*. At one elementary school talent show, I even played a little boogie-woogie.

Children feel joy and spontaneity and exhilaration when they make music, yet those emotions often disappear when formal music training begins. Music training today, I feel, too often emphasizes technique and musicianship while overlooking composition and improvisation. Somewhere a balance should be struck.

Improvisation offers perhaps the best opportunity to express personal creativity. Mozart, Liszt and Keith Jarrett are all recognized as *incredible* improvisers as well as great composers and performers. Ideally, music education should help children not only become musicians, but also creators. They should feel just as eager and proud playing their own creations as they would playing the music of a favorite composer. The ideal is to inspire children to *want* to play so that learning is a joy. Passion for learning and creating are perhaps the most important ingredients you can nurture in any student. Once the passion flows, the muse emerges.

Photo by Mark Gubin

SHELDON MIROWITZ

It all began with Mrs. Small, and a yellow upright that stood against a wall of my kindergarten classroom. On my first day of class, Mrs. Small called us to attention by playing the piano. She played it to announce nap time; she played it for us to sing along; sometimes she played it just so we could listen. I think I fell in love that first day of kindergarten — a little bit with Mrs. Small, a little with the piano, and a lot with music itself.

I did little else during my first week of class but hover by the piano. Mrs. Small, concerned with my lack of interest in anything else, called my parents and suggested piano lessons. My parents knew little about music but were firm believers in Experts and Training. Soon I found myself at the St. Louis Institute of Music, sitting on the knee of Mr. Croxford, the institute's director. He was old, possessed a proper accent and, to a 4 year old, was somewhat forbidding. (Actually, he is quite warm and kind.) In his office, sitting at his black Steinway, we began to determine whether or not I had Talent. He played some notes, then I played some notes. It was decided that I should enroll in the Preparatory Program.

Within a week we had a piano in the den (a Gulbransen Spinet with mushy action and suburban furniture non-tone). That piano saw me through years of lessons, first with Wilma Kopecky at the Preparatory School (who gently taught me the discipline of music), then privately with St. Louis jazz great Herb Drury (who encouraged and fostered my love of music). It is still in the den of my parents' home in St. Louis. Each time I go back it is a little more out of tune. Of course, I play it nonetheless.

Photo by Judith Broggi

BOB READ

It's been a long path from playing *Down in the Valley* at that first piano recital to sitting today at the grand piano in my studio, practicing and writing. Often the path hasn't been focused on the piano. Many instruments and styles of music have attracted me along the way, and all of these influences have been valuable and stay with me to this day.

After that early encounter with the piano came the drums, my first band and rock music; at the same time, I also played clarinet in the school band and large ensemble. This all led to jazz and the saxophone, and I was caught — music would be my life's work. With so many musical threads running through me, the piano settled in as a constant: the perfect companion for my saxophone playing, my writing tool of choice.

When I went on to attend the New England Conservatory of Music, the piano and its vast sonic possibilities unfolded before me as I listened to Ravel's *Gaspard de la Nuit*, or George Crumb's *Music for a Summer Evening*, or Prokofiev, or Bach.... Ever since, I've been working toward a music that could hold all of these loves, all of these sounds — saxophones, jazz, rock music, drums, composition, recording, Ravel, synthesizers, the piano. And the piano, that constant, beckons to me more each day with its enormous palette, its power and flexibility, its generosity and its satisfying simplicity.

Photo by Irene Young

BRIAN MANN

When I was 3, my Dad put a piano in my room and an accordion in my lap. Over the years, I've had some wonderful teachers who have really opened my eyes and ears in new ways. I learned about the physiological and psychological aspects of performance from Professor Phil Cohen of the Montreal Conservatory, Baroque ornamentation from M'Lou Dietzer, and traditional jazz improvisation from Helene Mirsch. My most essential lessons, though, were when I learned about the importance of learning and the value of practice from my Dad.

For me, playing the piano is sometimes the only way I can get certain feelings out. As I improvise at the piano I try to establish a direct connection between my feelings and what I am playing. I try to let the music carry me from one feeling to another; sometimes from despair or an expression of life's pain to spiritual understanding and on to hope and, many times, joy.

I hope that as I learn to express my deepest emotions more purely, the listener will feel the connection and the joy we all share. Thank you to all my teachers.

Photo by Ferderbar Studios

ARIADNE

By IRA STE

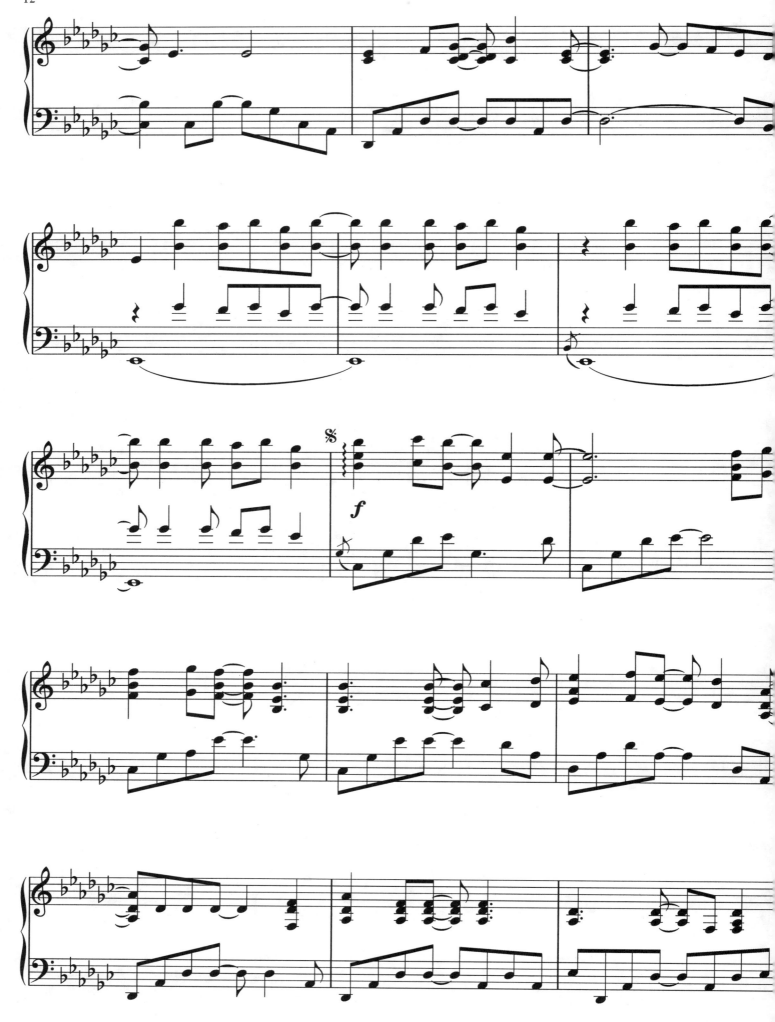

Improvise freely in D♭ Mixolydi

Continue improvising

Repeat ad lib.   C♭maj7#11

ASPEN SUMMER

By MICHAEL JONE

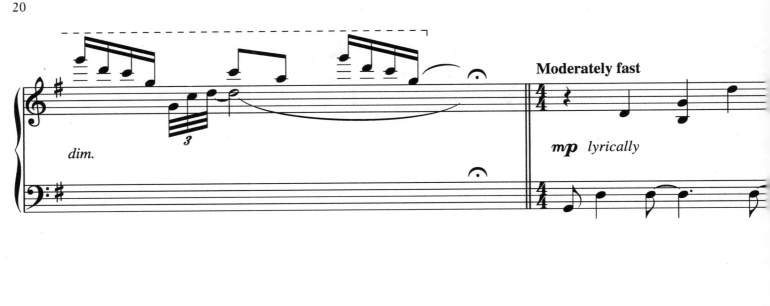

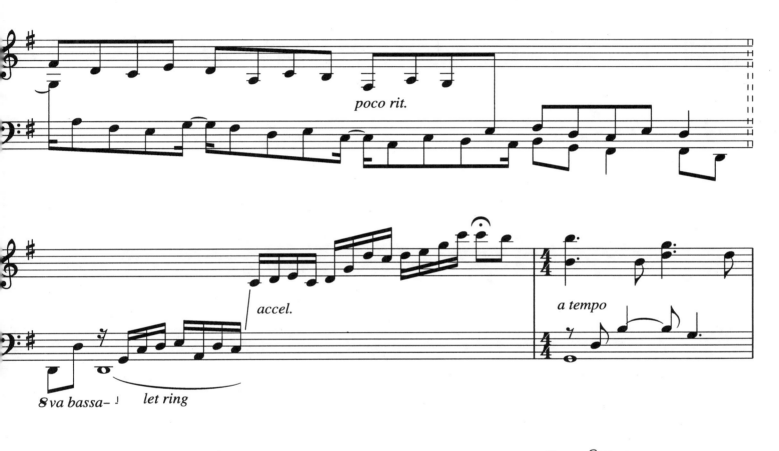

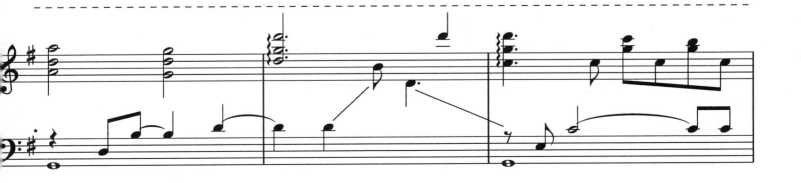

AUGUST 23rd, 1962

By SHELDON MIROWITZ

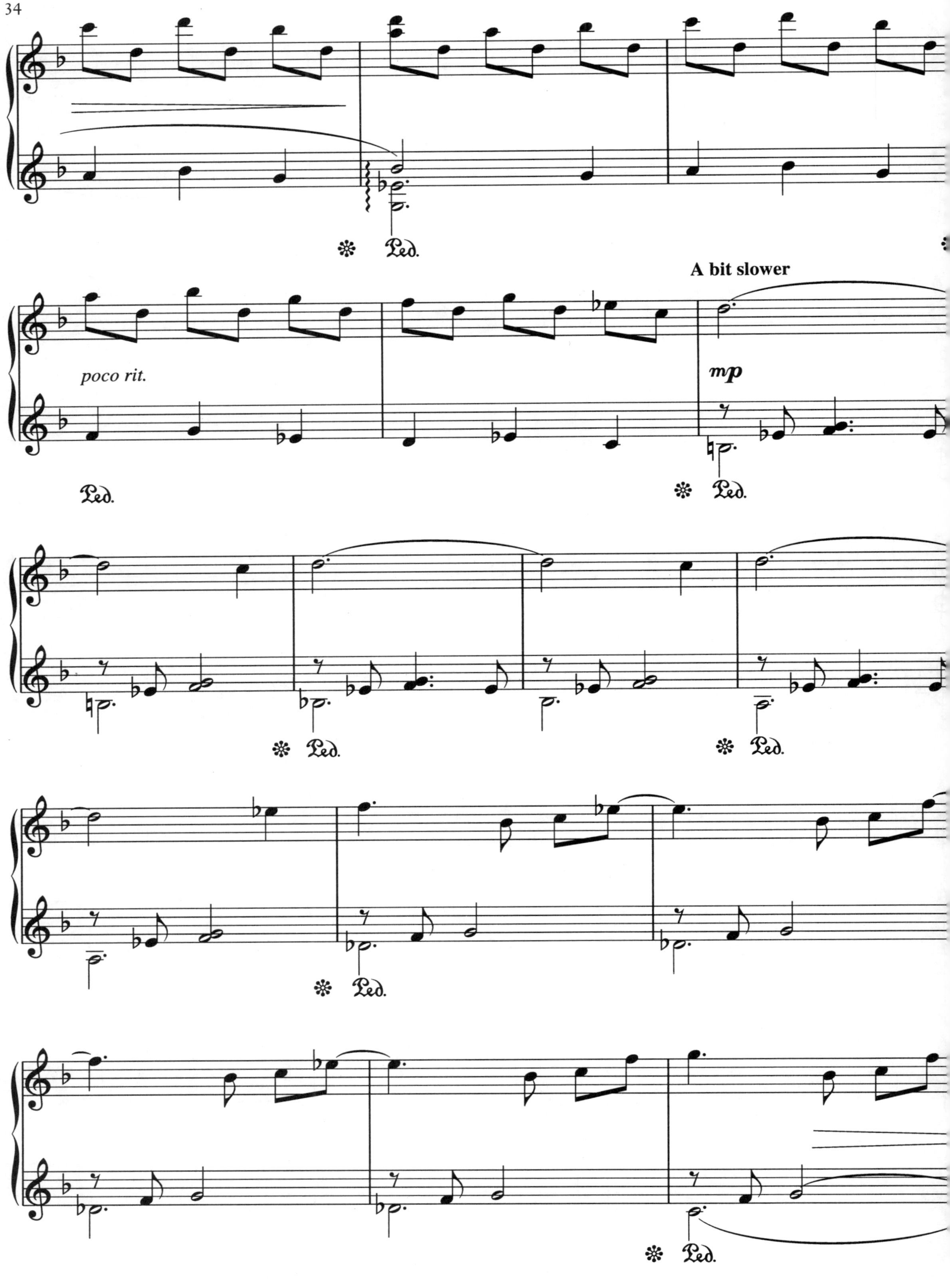

Ped.
A bit slower
poco rit.
mp
Ped.
Ped.
Ped.
Ped.
Ped.
Ped.

CYPRESS

By WAYNE GRATZ

Slowly and Freely

FIDDLETOWN

By IRA STEI

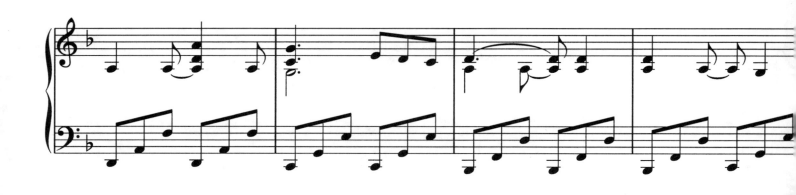

D.S. al Coda
(with repeat)

CODA

FLOWERS ON THE WATER

By KOST

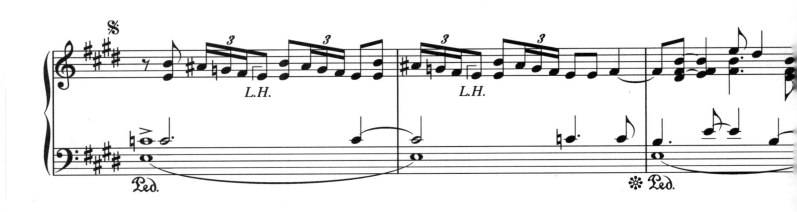

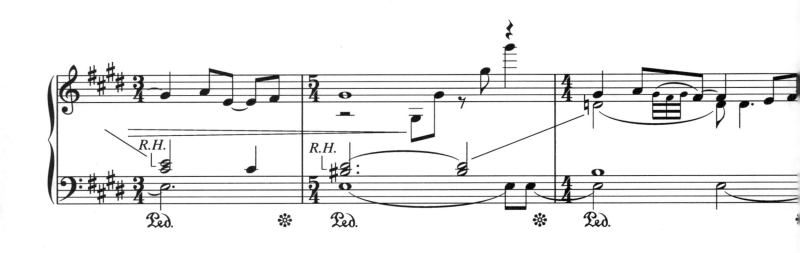

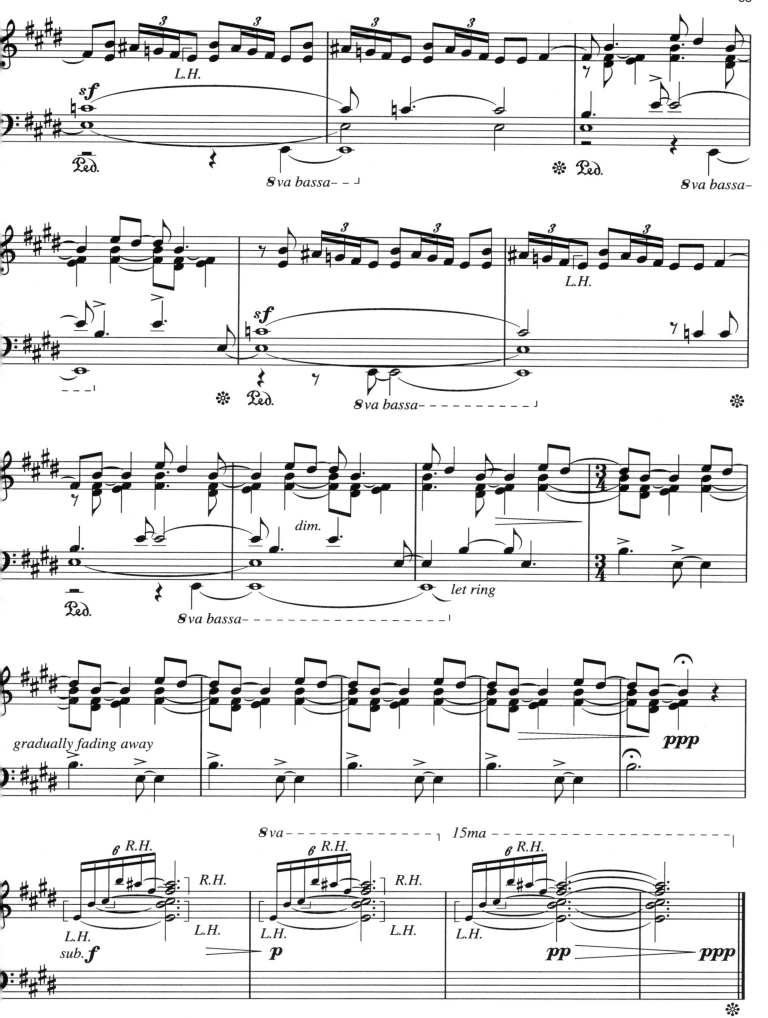

FIRST RAIN

By SPENCER BREWER

Quickly, lightly

With pedal throughout

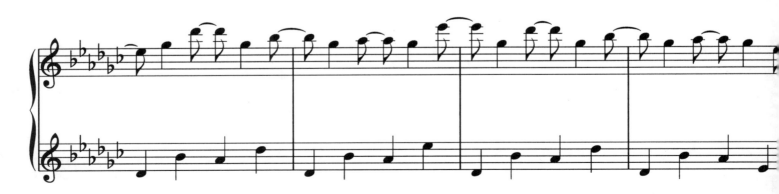

a tempo

58

GENTLE EARTH AND SKY

By MICHAEL GETTEL

With pedal throughout

To Coda ⊕

1.,3.

8va bassa - - ♩

GIRL FROM BARCELONA

By KOST

Gently, not too slow

With pedal throughout

Moderately, expressively

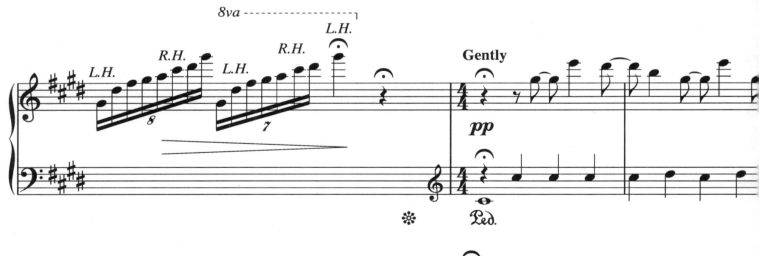

SO CLOSE

By WAYNE GRATZ

THE MEMORY

By NANCY RUMB

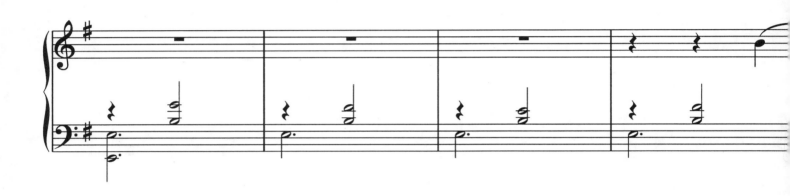

With motion

THE TEACHER

By BRIAN MAN

TURNING

By BOB READ

Swiftly, with a pulse

WHERE WE USED TO PLAY

By SPENCER BREW

A CATALOG OF NARADA RECORDINGS

NARADA LOTUS™
New Acoustic Music

N-61001	PIANOSCAPES Michael Jones
N-61002	SEASONS Gabriel Lee
N-61003	HEARTSOUNDS David Lanz
N-61004	SEASCAPES Michael Jones
N-61005	IMPRESSIONS Gabriel Lee
N-61006	NIGHTFALL David Lanz
N-61007	LOTUS SAMPLER #1 Narada Artists
N-61008	SOLSTICE David Lanz and Michael Jones
N-61009	SUNSCAPES Michael Jones
N-61010	OPENINGS William Ellwood
N-61011	EMERALD Brewer, Tingstad and Rumbel
N-61012	QUIET FIRE Ancient Future
N-61013	LOTUS SAMPLER #2 Narada Artists
N-61014	AMBER Michael Jones and David Darling
N-61015	RENAISSANCE William Ellwood
N-61016	WOODLANDS Tingstad, Rumbel and Lanz
N-61017	PORTRAITS Spencer Brewer
N-61018	LOTUS SAMPLER #3 Narada Artists
N-61019	DEPARTURES John Doan
N-61020	AFTER THE RAIN Michael Jones
N-61021	CRISTOFORI'S DREAM David Lanz
N-61022	LEGENDS Eric Tingstad and Nancy Rumbel
N-61023	REMINISCENCE Wayne Gratz
N-61024	VISTA William Ellwood
N-61025	LOTUS SAMPLER #4 Narada Artists
N-61026	HOMELAND Eric Tingstad and Nancy Rumbel
N-61027	MAGICAL CHILD Michael Jones
N-61028	PANORAMA Wayne Gratz
N-61029	WISDOM OF THE WOOD Narada Artists
N-61030	MORNING IN MEDONTE Michael Jones
N-61031	PIANO SOLOS Narada Artists
N-61032	GUITAR WORKS Narada Artists
N-61033	CAROUSEL Ira Stein

NARADA MYSTIQUE™
New Electronic Music

N-62001	VALLEY IN THE CLOUDS David Arkenstone
N-62002	THE WAITING Peter Buffett
N-62003	HIDDEN PATHWAYS Bruce Mitchell
N-62004	ONE BY ONE Peter Buffett
N-62005	A VIEW FROM THE BRIDGE Carol Nethen
N-62006	INTRUDING ON A SILENCE Colin Chin
N-62007	DANCING ON THE EDGE Bruce Mitchell
N-62008	CITIZEN OF TIME David Arkenstone
N-62009	MYSTIQUE SAMPLER ONE Narada Artists
N-62010	WARM SOUND IN A GRAY FIELD Peter Maunu
N-62011	THE MESSENGER Jim Jacobsen
N-62012	LOST FRONTIER Peter Buffett
N-62013	YONNONDIO Peter Buffett

NARADA EQUINOX.
New Age Fusion

N-63001	NATURAL STATES David Lanz and Paul Speer
N-63002	INDIAN SUMMER Friedemann
N-63003	DESERT VISION David Lanz and Paul Speer
N-63004	EQUINOX SAMPLER ONE Narada Artists
N-63005	ISLAND David Arkenstone with Andrew White
N-63006	CIRCLE Ralf Illenberger
N-63007	CROSS CURRENTS Richard Souther
N-63008	DORIAN'S LEGACY Spencer Brewer
N-63009	HEART & BEAT Ralf Illenberger
N-63010	MIL AMORES Doug Cameron
N-63011	MOON RUN Trapezoid
N-63012	CAFÉ DU SOLEIL Brian Mann
N-63013	WHITE LIGHT Martin Kolbe
N-63014	NEW LAND Bernardo Rubaja
N-63015	TWELVE TRIBES Richard Souther
N-63016	EQUINOX SAMPLER TWO Narada Artists
N-63017	AQUAMARINE Friedemann
N-63018	THE PIPER'S RHYTHM Spencer Brewer
N-63019	PLACES IN TIME Michael Gettel
N-63020	JOURNEY TO YOU Doug Cameron
N-63022	RHYTHM HARVEST The Michael Pluznick Group

NARADA COLLECTION SERIES.

N-39100	THE NARADA COLLECTION Narada Artists
N-39117	THE NARADA COLLECTION TWO Narada Artists
N-63902	THE NARADA CHRISTMAS COLLECTION Narada Artists
N-63904	THE NARADA NUTCRACKER Narada Artists
N-63905	THE NARADA WILDERNESS COLLECTION Narada Artists
N-63906	THE NARADA COLLECTION THREE Narada Artists
N-63907	A CHILDHOOD REMEMBERED Narada Artists
N-63908	ALMA DEL SUR Various Artists
N-63909	NARADA CHRISTMAS COLLECTION VOLUME 2 Narada Artists

NARADA ARTIST SERIES.

N-64001	SKYLINE FIREDANCE David Lanz
N-64002	MICHAEL'S MUSIC Michael Jones
N-64003	IN THE WAKE OF THE WIND David Arkenstone
N-64004	IN THE GARDEN Eric Tingstad and Nancy Rumbel
N-64005	RETURN TO THE HEART David Lanz
N-64006	THE SPIRIT OF OLYMPIA David Arkenstone and Kostia with David Lanz

NARADA CINEMA.

N-66001	MILLENNIUM: TRIBAL WISDOM AND THE MODERN WORLD Hans Zimmer
N-66002	COLUMBUS AND THE AGE OF DISCOVERY Sheldon Mirowitz
N-66003	SPACE AGE Jay Chattaway

Narada appreciates the support of our listeners, and we welcome your comments about the music of our artists.
Narada publishes a free, semi-annual newsletter that features personal interviews with Narada artists as well as information on new recordings.
You may receive future copies by writing to us and joining our growing, worldwide family of quality-minded listeners.

Please write to:
Friends of Narada, 1845 N. Farwell Avenue, Milwaukee, WI 53202 USA, *or*
Friends of Narada, P.O. Box 2301, 1200 CH Hilversum, Netherlands.